Love Letters
From the Great I Am

SHANNON ALEXANDER

WestBow Press books may be ordered through booksellers or by contacting:

WestBow Press
A Division of Thomas Nelson & Zondervan
1663 Liberty Drive
Bloomington, IN 47403
www.westbowpress.com
1 (866) 928-1240

ISBN: 978-1-5127-4863-5 (sc)
ISBN: 978-1-5127-4864-2 (e)

Library of Congress Control Number: 2016910864

Print information available on the last page.

WestBow Press rev. date: 07/27/2016

WestBow
PRESS®
A DIVISION OF THOMAS NELSON
& ZONDERVAN

Contents

My Testimony

I want to tell you my story. As a little girl (I think I might have been 6 or 7 years old) I made a conscious decision to be the best version of myself. So, as my life progressed I began to feel like a super hero in a dark city fighting injustice alone in a big bad world. I will be 40 years old this year and I just came to Christ in early winter. What that means is that while I was walking my dogs, I asked Jesus for forgiveness of my sins I invited Christ into my soul and thanked him for dying on the cross for me so that I could know God. It was an experiment really; I thought I have nothing to lose and eternity to gain. I thought what's the worst thing that could happen? Nothing right?

A few years ago a girl came to my house trying to sell us something we didn't need. She told me that she was hungry and asked for granola bar, so I invited her in to eat supper with us, (spaghetti) my husband thought I'd lost my mind! Well, I remember seeing a picture of Jesus Christ knocking on the door to a house with no doorknob. Would I let him into my house? Of course! We would have a feast! I imagined Him knocking on the door of my heart and I opened my heart to Him. The veil was lifted. It's all real heaven, God, Jesus Christ, the Holy Spirit, hell and the devil.

Little did I know that I, a super hero girl, just join the league of superheroes, with Jesus Christ as my leader. Just by asking him in, my world flipped upside down and backwards! I have witnessed many daily miracles since.

May God bless you on this day the Lord has made.

One of my favourite Bible passages is this:
Romans 5:19 "For as by one man's disobedience many were made sinners, so also by one Man's obedience many will be made righteous." – Jesus Calling Devotional Bible – New King James Version

It is a favourite passage of mine because it really illustrates the grand scale of mankind's story so far…

My Story Continues...

Once Jesus Christ had arrived in my heart I felt lead by the Holy Spirit that I had to write and paint. I'd always loved to write and draw when I was a girl but the pressures of life seem to get in the way. God's purpose for me became clear, I needed to write and paint with God through the Holy Spirit within me. So I made an agreement with the Lord to write every night.

I have written this book believing that the Father, the Son, and the Holy Spirit are one however they have different perspectives. The Holy Spirit resides in me and the rest of the body of Christ and is connected to Jesus Christ (Yeshua) who is my King and Savior and He is connected to the Father, who is the Creator God Almighty (Yahweh).

Finally, in parenthesis I have included the color of pen that I chose to write with at that time as a point of interest. My Aunt in Washington had suggested I buy a red pen; so I went to the stationary store and found a red pen, a gold pen, a pink pen and a silver pen and bought all of them! When I got home I discovered that the brand name of the pens was "Cross". I smiled and looked up and began my journey. Please enjoy.

The Baptism

It is a great thing to be a part of the living waters they flow from Me to you and from you to the multitude. The waters are alive! The word is alive! I impart great grace in the waters. It is with love that you come to Me and I to you. As a father who longed for the return of his beloved child. I hold you in the palm of my hand and smile. You are a prized jewel in heaven and have a home in My Kingdom, my beloved Little One.

(Gold Pen)

To you, I have looked so far ahead. I knew you, thousands of years before you were born; your soul, I knew, belong to Me. I gladly died, not for your sin but because of your virtue. It is your virtue, the purest most perfect part of your soul, I died for. The price for your sin was my life and I would do it all over again to know you would choose Me and my Father in Heaven. Welcome my Beloved.

(Red Pen)
Glory in the highest!
Hallelujah!

Amen

Isaiah 12: 3-4
"With joy you will draw water from the springs of salvation. At that time, you will say. 'Praise God (Yahweh). Call on his name. Make his deeds known among the nations. Make them remember that his name is highly honored.'" – Names of God Bible – God's Word Translation.

"I baptize you with water so that you will change the way you think and act. But the one who comes after me is more powerful than I. I am not worthy to remove his sandals. He will baptize you with the Holy Spirit and fire." - Names of God Bible – God's Word Translation

Love

Love is what breaks the chains of intolerance. It finds a way to bridge the differences between people and binds us closer together. Like a river it flows into us, over us, and through us. Carving the very nature of our being like the pebbles on the riverbed. Without love, we shrivel and our hearts become hardened and our lives flat-line. With love, the essence of life is vibrant and three-dimensional. You'll find no greater love than God in Heaven's love, it is without flaw. My love is without flaw and the Holy Spirit's love is without flaw. It is perfect and it can be found in the Great I AM just look up.

For His Father's creations
(Red Pen)

1 Chronicles 16:34
"Give thanks to the Lord, for he is good; for his love endures forever!" – Holy Bible – King James Version

1 Corinthians 13:1, 13:4-7
"I may speak in the languages of humans and of angels. But if I don't have love, I am but a loud gong or a clashing cymbal…Love is patient. Love is kind. Love isn't jealous. It doesn't sing its own praises. It isn't arrogant. It isn't rude. It doesn't think about itself. It isn't irritable. It doesn't keep track of wrongs. It isn't happy when injustice is done, but it is happy with the truth. Love never stops being patient, never stops believing, never stops hoping, never gives up." – Names of God Bible – God's Word Translation

Your Voice

Your voice is decadent like the finest of wine and richest of sauces. It is the sweetest of scents and the boldest of colours. Your voice is the softest of wool and wraps me up in velvety comfort. It is tender at times and full of authority at others. The vibrations of it fills my soul with your power like the roar of a tiger. You are the King and I adore your voice within me.

I pray you never leave me. That you never grow silent. That I may follow the voice of my shepherd, you Yeshua (Jesus Christ), forever. If I stumble or go astray please bring me back, cleanse my soul, and help me through my trials as you have so many times before. I am willing to follow you, I know I have the courage to do so, most of the time. If I don't have the courage, I pray you provide what I need.

Thank you.

Amen.

Love Shannon
(Silver Pen)

Revelations 3:20-22

"Look, I'm standing at the door and knocking. If anyone listens to my voice and opens the door, I'll come in and we'll eat together. I will allow everyone who wins the victory to sit with me on my throne, as I have won the victory and have sat down with my Father on his throne. Let the person who has ears to listen to what the Spirit says to the churches." - Names of God Bible – God's Word Translation.

John 10:3-5

"The gatekeeper opens the gate for him, and the sheep respond to his voice. He calls his sheep by name and leads them out of the pen. After he has brought out all of his sheep, he walks ahead of them. The sheep follow him because they recognize his voice. They won't follow a stranger because they don't recognize his voice." – Names of God Bible – God's Word Translation.

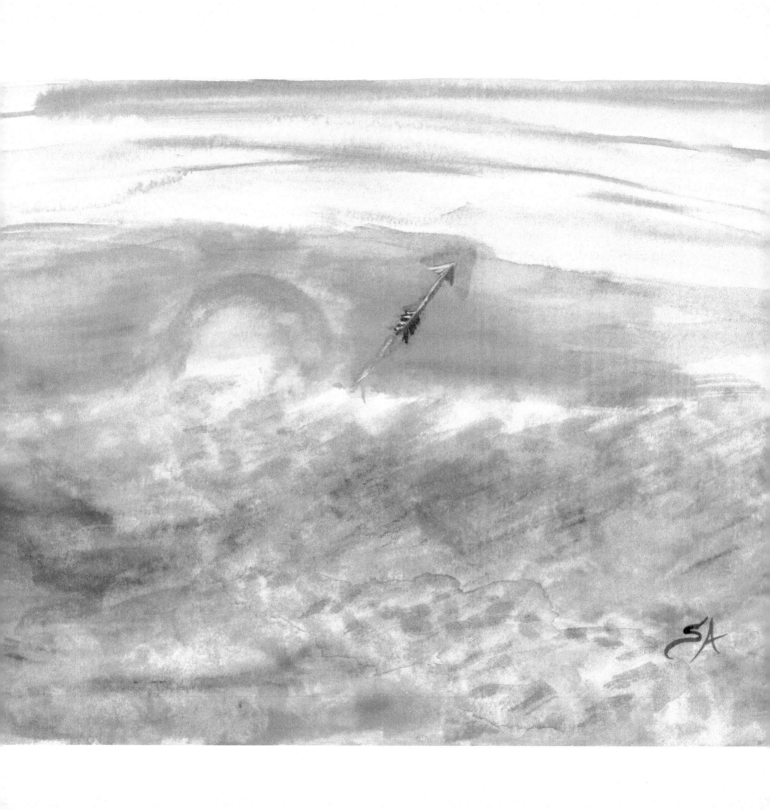

Arrow

et my arrow fly steady and true. The shaft of truth strong and slender. The butt a foundation of faith. With feathers of peace and a head of love, let it fly a course that will break the chains that shackle us. Let my arrow bring God's freedom!

(Pink Pen)

Matthew 28:18-20
"And Jesus came and spoke to them, saying, 'All authority has been given to Me in heaven and on earth. Go therefore and make disciples of all the nations, baptizing them in the name of the Father and of the Son and of the Holy Spirit, teaching them to observe all things that I have commanded you; and lo, I am with you always, even to the end of the age.' Amen" – Jesus Calling Devotional Bible – New King James Version

Technicolor Eyes

My brilliant blue eyes behold the world.
I see dewdrops forming like pearls on a leaf.
I see leaves in the brilliant sun shimmer and quake in the wind.
I see bark on the trees like wrinkles of a man.
I see the shoots of grass sway compliantly with the wind.
I see the horizon where the earth meets the sky.
I see the sun dipped low beyond the earth.
I see stars' pop out into the night sky like wild flowers popping up high on a mountain plateau.
I see the full round moon pregnant with light that fills the starry heaven.
These are true treasures, all of the rich men seek them but never have time to find them.
We need only to see in Technicolor.
(Gold Pen)

Genesis 1:31
"Then God saw everything that He made, and indeed it was very good. So the evening and the morning were the sixth day." Jesus Calling Devotional Bible – New King James Version

The African Storm

Plump droplets fall from the luminous clouds. The rhythm is slow at first. The heavy droplets bounce off the parched land. Like a desperate animal, the land cries for the moisture of life. In response, the clouds release their burden as if God in heaven has heard the call of the land. The water brings life; a new one of lush greenery and migrating herds. It is a struggle of survival for many creatures whom depend on the mercy of God. The lightening cracks and a bolt of fearful joy tears through the hearts of many. For they anticipate the arrival of a new season that brings with it new opportunities. As water flows so too does life.

(Red Pen)

Zachariah 10:1
"Ask Yahweh (God) for rain in the springtime Yahweh makes thunderstorms. He gives everyone rain showers for the plants in the field" - Names of God Bible – God's Word Translation

Serenity

As far as the oceans wide.
As tall as the mighty mountain peaks.
My love for you is abound.
I lift you up for you to find serenity.

As tranquil as the fresh dewy forest.
As peaceful as a glassy lake at sunset.
Rest in me to find serenity.

Follow Me quietly.
Our secret life of miracles.
Hand in hand you walk the path of serenity.

(Pink Pen)

Ezekiel 34:25-26
"I will make a covenant of peace with them, and cause wild beasts to cease from the land; they will dwell safely in the wilderness and sleep in the woods. I will make them and the places all around My hill a blessing; and I will cause showers to come down in their season; there shall be showers of blessing."
Jesus Calling Devotional Bible – New King James Version

My Little Boat

Her little sailboat slices through the waves. Against the odds the little woman prays. She remains solidly rooted in her magnificent Lord. Her sails are guided by Elohim's breath. She smiles brightly in anticipation of His tests. The joy and the thrill of I AM's adventure make her eyes open wide in awe of her Lord forever more.

(Pink Pen)

Mark 4:35-36

"On the same day, when evening had come, He said to them, 'Let's cross to the other side.' Now when they had left the multitude, they took Him along in the boat as He was. ..." Jesus Calling Devotional Bible – New King James Version

Forging Fire

Tonight the candles glow bright.
The trumpets will sound.
The celebration will ensue...

Burn bright, burn low, let the Holy Spirit flow.
The fire will forge a newly transformed beauty.
Her soul is new she has changed her view.
Nothing will ever be the same again.

(Pink Pen)

Luke 3 – John Prepares the Way (This is John the Baptist being referenced)
Luke 3:16
"John answered, saying to all, 'I indeed baptize you with water; but One mightier than I is coming, whose sandal strap I am not worthy to loose. He will baptize you with the Holy Spirit and fire.'"
Jesus Calling Devotional Bible – New King James Version

Acts 2 – Believers Are filled with the Holy Spirit
Acts 2:1-4
"When Pentecost, the fiftieth day after Passover, came, all the believers were together in one place. Suddenly, a sound like a violently blowing wind came from the sky and filled the whole house where they were staying. Tongues that looked like fire appeared to them. The tongues arranged themselves so that one came to rest on each believer. All the believers were filled with the Holy Spirit and began to speak in other languages as the Spirit gave them the ability to speak." Names of God Bible – God's Word Translation

One Step at a Time

Can a turtle take too long?
Will the songbird sing her song?
Together we go through eternity one step at a time.

Blow wind blow and cleanse this land.
The sun will shine upon the sand.
Together we grow and change,
one step at a time.

As her hand sets forth to do my bidding.
Her artistic touch is fitting.
Together we create one step at a time.

Her soul drinks up the water of life,
allowing her to take one step at a time.

(Pink Pencil)

Matthew 5:14-16
"You are the light of the world. A city that is set on a hill cannot be hidden. Nor do they light a lamp and put it under a basket, but on a lamp stand, and it gives light to all who are in the house. Let your light so shine before men, that they may see your good works and glorify your Father in heaven." - Jesus Calling Devotional Bible – New King James Version

Veil

Sunset and storm clouds reveal veils of iridescent light from heaven. Like big beautiful pillars across the fields of wheat and barley.

On the long winding trail, I asked Him into my heart and soul. Asking for forgiveness of my past poor decisions… and… the veil was lifted! I was no longer blind and my ears were clear. I could hear King Jesus and I could see the good and evil in the world I never fully understood existed.

The very best veil is placed upon her head. The tiniest pearls shining in the everlasting light covers her face as she walks down the aisle toward her groom of everlasting life, her King, her Love, Yeshua.

(Pink Pen)

2 Corinthians 3: 12-18
"Since we have confidence in the new promise we speak boldly. We are not like Moses. He kept covering his face with a veil. He didn't want the people of Israel to see the glory fading away. However, their minds became closed. In fact, to this day the same veil is still there when they read the old Testament. It isn't removed, because only Christ can remove it. Yet, even today, when they read the books of Moses, a veil covers their minds. But whenever a person turns to the Lord, the veil is taken away. This Lord is the Spirit. Wherever the Lord's Spirit is, there is freedom. As all of us reflect the Lord's glory with faces that are not covered with veils, we are being changed into his image with ever-increasing glory. This comes from the Lord, who is the Spirit." - Names of God Bible – God's Word
Translation

Revelation 19:6-8
"…'Alleluia! For the Lord God Omnipotent reigns! Let us be glad and rejoice and give Him glory, for the marriage of the lamb has come and His wife has made herself ready.' And to her it was granted to be arrayed in fine linen, clean and bright, for the fine linen is the righteous acts of the saints." – Jesus Calling Devotional Bible – New King James Version

The Broken Bird

She flies amidst the hurricane. Being born into a cruel world her parents are broken before she even learns how to fly. Her heart is golden within her chest but bit by bit the brightness fades. She is a valiant bluebird brave and kind. Soon she grows tired of the relentless wind that carries her far from home. Her little wings beat fiercely and her heart flutters wildly within her chest as her body is thrown against the high sharp cliffs.

In the quiet, she barely breathes she takes in life moment by moment, gracefully. It is then she looks up waiting to see the eyes of her Maker. The bird, so bright and blue, is broken. Her soul, a beautiful rare gem of the sky. She has never known her beauty; she has never known her value.

Bent and broken, she is feather-light in the hand of the Lord. He smiles and pours His love into her. Her heart glows more brightly than ever before. Bit by bit, all of her pain and brokenness is revealed and then healed by the Lord Jesus Christ. This little bird will fly again and know the joy and the love of God.

(Pink Pen)

Isaiah 35 – The Lord's People Will Have Joy (I personally enjoy the entire chapter, it's worth a read☺)
Isaiah 35: 3-4
"Strengthen limp hands. Steady weak knees. Tell those who are terrified, 'be brave; don't be afraid. Your Elohim (God) will come with vengeance, with divine revenge. He will come and rescue you.'" – Names of God Bible – God's Word Translation

Isaiah 35:10
"The people ransomed by Yahweh (God) will return. They will come to Zion singing with joy. Everlasting happiness will be on their heads as a crown. They will be glad and joyful. They will have no sorrow or grief." - Names of God Bible – God's Word Translation

The Cooks in the Kitchen

A five-star chef has come to town. He is not just any chef, He is the master chef, known throughout the land. Each of us have a kitchen designed and built differently from one another. Some of us ask the chef to come over and teach us to cook, for we are city of people who love to cook and eat. He will accept our invitation if our hearts are genuine. When He comes in we design a recipe, the unique five-star dish that only our kitchen can make, we attempt to cook...

However, our grease traps are full and our pantries are a mess! We have rotten food in the fridge from long ago. The master chef, He identifies parts of our kitchen that need work. He waits for us to work with Him. Are we going to be prideful and become angry with Him? Are we going to fall apart and leave weeping, condemning ourselves for the shabby condition of our kitchen? Are we going to find excuses to do something else because it's to difficult and uncomfortable? Or are we going to asked for directions from Him get some degreasers, throw some food out of the fridge to make room for the fresh bounty from the local market, and get some shelving and a label maker for the pantry? He wants to teach us the secrets of His kitchen but we have to be honest with Him. We need to put away our ego and pride believing our kitchen is perfect when it's not. So we make a list of things to be thrown away and organized and cleansed. We make a list of the new tools we need to accomplish for our signature dish. Together we clean, we replace and transform the kitchen. Now the stage is set to create a masterpiece with the master chef.

Can you already taste your signature dish that will impact the world? What type of spices are you going to use? Are you filled with joy and excitement at the thought of creating a new dish, and doing what you are meant to do, working with the five-star chef to do it? Your kitchen is clean and now the world is yours to co-create the five-star chef, whose name incidentally happens to be Jesus Christ. Your kitchen is your heart and your signature dish is what God put you on this planet to do. Your signature dish is uniquely yours and a vibrant piece of the woven tapestry.

Love Shannon
(Silver Pen)

Titus 2:14
"He gave himself for us to set us free from every sin and to cleanse us so that we can be his special people who are enthusiastic about doing good things." Names of God Bible – God's Word Translation

Phillippians 4:11-13
"I'm not saying this because I'm in any need. I've learned to be content in whatever situation I'm in. I know how to live in poverty or prosperity. No matter what the situation, I've learned the secret of how to live when I'm full or when I'm hungry, when I have too much or when I have too little. I can do everything through Christ who strengthens me." Names of God Bible – God's Word Translation

Train Station

I arrive on the black hardened platform of the train station. My baggage way too large and heavy to carry. I push, pull, and drag my burdens. They weigh me down and my soul is scarred, saddened and I am exhausted. On this cloudy, rainy day I stop in front of you, Yeshua (God). Tears stream down my face and my head hangs low after what seems to be a long, arduous, and painful journey. I look up into your serene face with hope. Please take these burdens from me. Please heal me, my King. He smiles and my heart lifts. He picks up my baggage as though it was light as feathers and places it on the train. He holds my hand and we walk off the train to the other side into a meadow. I hear the train pull away from the station with my burdens on it. The train is gone and my soul is safely in the hands of Jesus.

Love Shannon
(Silver Pen)

Matthew 9:9-12 – Jesus Chooses Matthew to Be a Disciple
"When Yeshua (Jesus Christ) was leaving that place, he saw a man sitting in a tax office. The man's name was Matthew. Yeshua said to him, 'Follow Me!' So Matthew got up and followed him. Later Yeshua was having dinner at Matthew's house. Many tax collectors and sinners came to eat with Yeshua and his disciples. The Pharisees saw this and asked his disciples, 'why does your teacher eat with tax collectors and sinners?' When Yeshua heard that, he said, 'Healthy people don't need a doctor; those who are sick do. Learn what this means: 'I want mercy, not sacrifices.' I've come to call sinners, not people who think they have God's approval.'" – The Names of God Bible – God's Word Translation

My thoughts on this…
Like the man hanging on the cross next to Jesus Christ said, "Our punishment is fair. We are getting what we deserve. But this man hasn't done anything wrong." And Jesus responds, "I can guarantee this truth: Today you will be with me in paradise." I think that in order to receive life from Christ we need to humble ourselves enough to see our own faults (sins) and understand the goodness of God asking and receiving forgiveness so that we can do the same with the people we love who surround us.

A Flower in the Quiet

In the quiet of the garden in a secluded place grows a special rose. She is soft, velvet and fragrant. Her beauty is impressive. Many passed by her, but God knows where she grows. He knows this hidden treasure for He put her there. He calls her forth to grow in His royal garden and sends His caretaker for her.

Love Shannon
(Silver Pen)

Matthew 5:5
"Blessed are the meek, for they shall inherit the earth." – Jesus Calling Devotional Bible – New King James Version

Thank you to my friends, family, and neighbours who have helped me along the way. Most of all, I thank the Great I AM for *all* of my blessings. Amen. Love Shannon

CPSIA information can be obtained
at www.ICGtesting.com
Printed in the USA
LVOW06s1731150916

504772LV00039B/239/P